This book belongs to

....

Quarto Knows

Quarto is the authority on a wide range of topics.

Quarto educates, entertains and enriches the lives of our readers—enthusiasts and lovers of hands-on living.

www.quartoknows.com

First published in 2019 by QED Publishing,
an imprint of The Quarto Group.
The Old Brewery, 6 Blundell Street,
London N7 9BH, United Kingdom.
T (0)20 7700 6700 F (0)20 7700 8066
www.QuartoKnows.com

A catalogue record for this book is available from the British Library.

ISBN 978-1-78603-608-7

Based on the original story by Peter Bently and Duncan Beedle

Author of adapted text: Katie Woolley
Series Editor: Joyce Bentley
Series Designer: Sarah Peden

Manufactured in Dongguan, China TL112018

9 8 7 6 5 4 3 2 1

FSC
www.fsc.org
MIX
Paper from responsible sources
FSC® C104723

Reading Gems

Zipp! Zapp!

QED

Focus sounds in this book

f
fix

ff
hu**ff**

j
jam

l
f**l**oss

ll
hi**ll**

pp
za**pp**

qu
Planet **Qu**ip

ss
hi**ss**

v
visit

w
we

x
fi**x**

y
yes

z
zapp

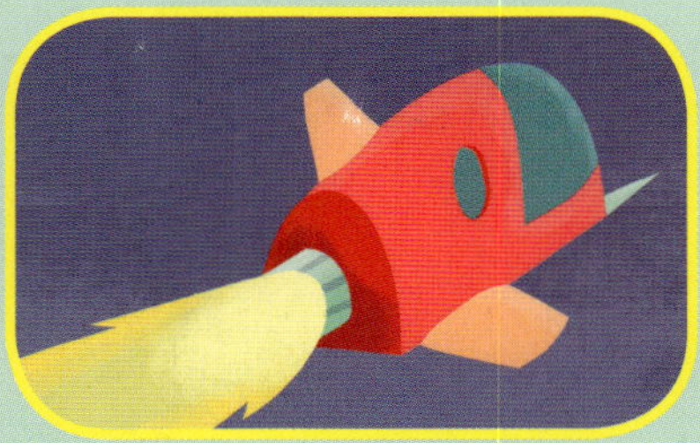

zz
bu**zz**

The bugs.

Nid, San and Pem visit Gop.

She has got a Zipp Zapp!

Nid got the Zipp Zapp.

Huff!
Hiss!
POP!

The pots and pans got stuck to Nid.

The tins got stuck to Nid.

He was in a jam.

Gop got the Zipp Zapp back.

Can she fix Nid?

Yes, she can!

The bugs got the pots
and pans back.

The bugs can go to visit the mud vubs.

The bugs buzz off to Planet Quip.

The mud vubs dab and floss.

The bugs dab and floss.

Mess and mud!

The bugs jet off to go back to bed. Buzz! No!

The rocket is stuck on a hill.

Can it be fixed?

Yes, Gop can zap the hill!

She can fix it.

The rocket is not stuck.

Quick! Gop gets into the rocket!

The rocket has shot off the hill.

Buzz! Pop!

Will the bugs go to bed?

No. A mud vub is in the rocket.

The bugs must go back to Planet Quip.

Let's Talk About Zipp! Zapp!

Look at the back cover.

Point to the focus letters.

Can you make the letter sounds?

Can you find the tricky words 'no' and 'into' in the story?

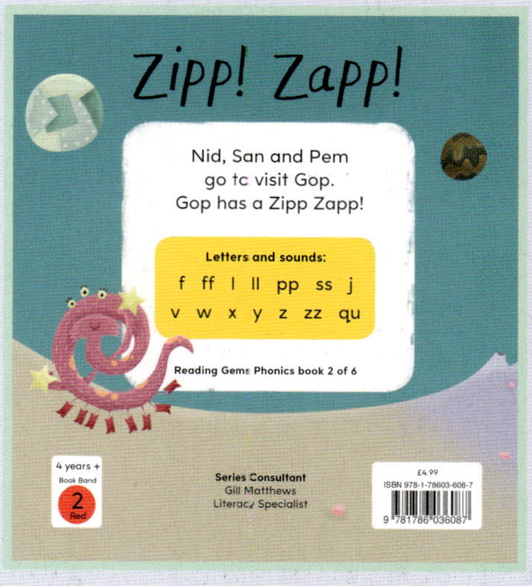

Point to the letter 'f' in the word 'fix'.

What sound does 'f' make?

Can you find some other words in the story with the letter 'f' in them?

Can you think of any other words with 'i' in them?

Find the letters 'qu' at the beginning of 'Quip'.

Can you sound out the whole name?

What other space objects can you see in this picture?

Why did Nid want the Zipp Zapp?

What happened when he played with it?

Who helped Nid?

How did Gop help?

Did you like the story about Gop and her Zipp Zapp?

What was your favourite bit?

Fun and Games

Find the word that begins with the correct letter sound to complete these sentences.

f

fix | stuck | zapp

Yes, Gop can ..... Nid!

Qu

Quip | lit | wick

The bugs go to Planet ..... .

j

jet | go | up

The bugs ..... off to visit the mud vubs.

Answers: f: fix; Qu: **Quip** and j: jet.

Z

Zapp | gap | tap

Gop has a Zipp ..... .

Find the word that ends with the correct letter sound to complete these sentences.

ll

hill | pop | flop

The ..... can go hiss.

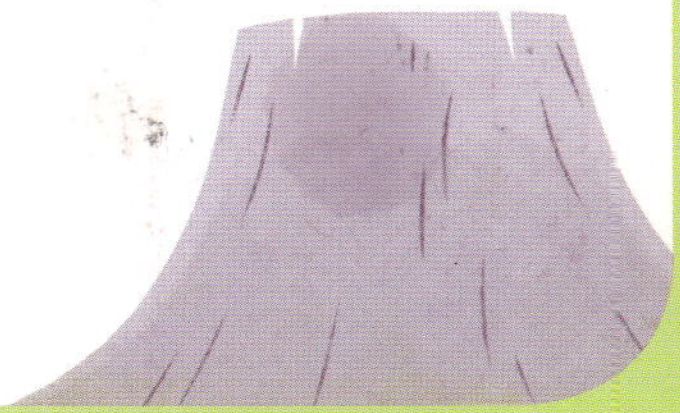

ss

floss | plop | tap

The mud vubs
dab and ..... .

Answers: Z: **Zapp**; ll: **hill** and ss: **floss**.

Reading With Your Little Bugs

Here are some tips to help you enjoy reading this book with your child.

1. Encourage your child to read the story to you, saying the sounds and putting them together to read the word.

2. If your child gets stuck on a word, show them how to break it down into sounds.

3. Have fun! You could make up silly voices for each of the characters and even act out the story together.

4. Remember to give your child lots of praise!

5. If your child is starting to feel tired or bored, put the book away and pick it up another day.

Mind-Boggling Phonics Glossary

Phonics often feels a bit confusing, with lots of alien terms. This glossary will help demystify Phonics!

blend to put individual sounds together to read a word, e.g. s-n-a-p blended together reads 'snap'.

CVC word a word spelled with a consonant, then a vowel, then a consonant, like 'sat' or 'tip'.

decode to put sounds and letters together to read a word correctly.

digraph two letters representing one sound, e.g. ck in 'kick'.

grapheme a letter or group of letters representing one sound, e.g. t, b, sh, ch, igh, ough (as in 'though').

phoneme a single unit of sound, e.g. the letter 't' represents just one sound and the letters 'sh' represent just one sound.

segment to split up a word into its individual phonemes in order to spell, e.g. the word 'cat' has three phonemes: /c/ /a/ /t/.

sight words or high-frequency words are words that appear most often in printed materials. They may not be decodable using phonics (or too advanced) but they are useful to learn separately by sight to develop fluency in reading.

tricky words are words that cannot be sounded out with phonics, such as 'the', 'was' and 'one'. Sometimes called exception words.

trigraph three letters representing one sound, e.g. igh in 'night'.

GET TO KNOW READING GEMS

Reading Gems is a series of books that has been written for children who are learning to read. The books have been created in consultation with a literacy specialist.

The books fit into five levels, with each level getting more challenging as a child's confidence and reading ability grows. The simple text and fun illustrations provide gradual, structured practice of reading. Most importantly, these books are good stories that are fun to read!

Phonics is for children who are learning their letters and sounds. Simple, engaging stories provide gentle phonics practice.

Level 1 is for children who are taking their first steps into reading. Story themes and subjects are familiar to young children, and there is lots of repetition to build reading confidence.

Level 2 is for children who have taken their first reading steps and are becoming readers. Story themes are still familiar but sentences are a bit longer, as children begin to tackle more challenging vocabulary.

Level 3 is for children who are developing as readers. Stories and subjects are varied, and more descriptive words are introduced.

Level 4 is for readers who are rapidly growing in reading confidence and independence. There is less repetition on the page, broader themes are explored and plot lines straddle multiple pages.

Phonics